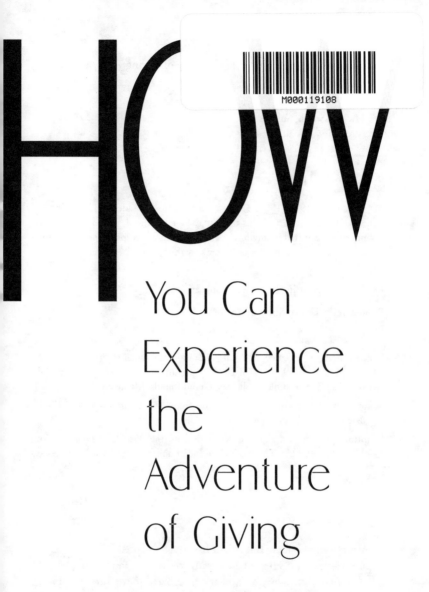

How

You Can Experience the Adventure of Giving

BILL BRIGHT

How You Can Experience the Adventure of Giving

Published by
Campus Crusade for Christ
375 Hwy 74 South, Suite A
Peachtree City, GA 30269

ISBN 1-56399-110-1

Design and typesetting by Genesis Publications.

Printed in the United States of America.

Unless otherwise indicated, Scripture quotations are taken from the *New International Version*, © 1973, 1978, 1984 by the International Bible Society. Published by Zondervan Bible Publishers, Grand Rapids, Michigan.

Scripture quotations designated TLB are from *The Living Bible*, © 1971 by Tyndale House Publishers, Wheaton, Illinois.

Scripture quotations designated NKJ are from the *New King James* version, © 1979, 1980, 1982 by Thomas Nelson Inc., Publishers, Nashville, Tennessee.

As a personal policy, Bill Bright has never accepted honorariums or royalties for his personal use. Any royalties from this book are dedicated to the glory of God and designated to the various ministries of Campus Crusade for Christ.

What Is a Transferable Concept?

When our Lord commanded the eleven men with whom He had most shared His earthly ministry to go into all the world and make disciples of all nations, He told them to teach these new disciples all that He had taught them (Matthew 28:18–20).

Later the apostle Paul gave the same instructions to Timothy: "The things you have heard me say in the presence of many witnesses entrust to reliable men who will also be qualified to teach others" (2 Timothy 2:2).

In the process of counseling and interacting with tens of thousands of students, laymen, and pastors since 1951, our staff have discovered the following:

- Many church members (including people from churches that honor our Lord and faithfully teach His Word) are not sure of their salvation.

- The average Christian is living a defeated and frustrated life.

- The average Christian does not know how to share his faith effectively with others.

In our endeavor to help meet these three basic needs and to build Christian disciples, Campus Crusade for Christ has developed a series of "how to's"—or "transferable concepts"—in which we discuss many of the basic truths that Jesus and His disciples taught.

A "transferable concept" is an idea or a truth that can be transferred or communicated from one person to another and then to another, spiritual generation after generation, without distorting or diluting its original meaning.

As these basic truths—"transferable concepts"—of the Christian life are made available through the printed word, films, video tapes, and audio cassettes in every major language of the world, they could well be used of God to help transform the lives of tens of millions throughout the world.

We encourage you to master each of these concepts by reading it thoughtfully at least six times[1] until you are personally prepared to communicate it to others "who will also be qualified to teach others." By mastering these basic materials and discipling others to do the same, many millions of men and women can be reached and discipled for Christ and thus make a dramatic contribution toward the fulfillment of the Great Commission in our generation.

Bill Bright

---

[1] Educational research confirms that the average person can master the content of a concept, such as this one, by reading it thoughtfully six times.

Contents

HOW YOU CAN EXPERIENCE THE ADVENTURE OF GIVING

Preparing for the Adventure

What does the word "adventure" mean to you? Is it shooting the rapids on a hot summer day...

Or speeding around a race track at two hundred miles per hour...

Or climbing a sheer cliff in the Alps...

Or trekking through a wilderness on safari?

Permit me to share with you one of the most exciting adventures you can experience—the adventure of *giving by faith*.

Most people don't relate adventure to the act of giving. In the following pages, I want to show you how to turn your giving into a thrilling personal adventure. But first, let me tell you about Deborah, just one of God's children who has made this wonderful discovery.

Not long after returning to the United States from overseas missionary work, she learned that one of her neighbor's sons had been seriously injured. The family had no insurance and was suffering financially as well as physically.

Concerned about their urgent need, Deborah went into her bedroom to pray. "Lord," she asked, "what would You have me do?" She sensed a nudge from the Lord to give her neighbors some money. Checking her bank account, she realized that her bank balance was a mere $200.

"Lord, how about $25?" she prayed. With $175 left over, she thought she could survive the rest of the month. Quietly waiting on the Lord, however, she felt the Lord say, "No, I want you to give $100."

"I choked a bit," she says. "That was half of what I had. As I continued to question the Lord, I had no peace about anything less than $100."

Finally, she wrote out a check, breathing a prayer. "Lord, I've done what You said, so You'll have to take care of my needs."

With a sense of joy and expectancy, Deborah took the check across the street. By this act of sharing, she greatly encouraged the family, and God blessed her abundantly. Two days later a check for $100 came in the mail. Three days later a woman dropped by her home with a check for $200.

"Within five days of writing my check, I received from unexpected sources a total of $500," Deborah says. "I stood in awe of God and His ways."

Like Deborah and many other Christians who have learned to obey God's principles of stewardship, you can know and experience this wonderful adventure of giving by faith.

As with any adventure, we must prepare for our journey. In the next few pages, I want to share how you can equip yourself for your adventure. I urge you to read this booklet prayerfully and carefully, underlining significant points and making notes in the margins for quick, easy reference. Then pass these principles on to your spouse, a close friend, and other Christians you know, especially those you are discipling.

Understand Stewardship

To start on your adventure, you first must understand the meaning and importance of stewardship.

In the New Testament, two different words describe a steward. One emphasizes guardianship over children and the administration of a master's household. The other stresses the role of a manager over property. In either case, a steward over-sees the affairs and property of another person.

One cannot overemphasize the importance of steward-ship. Stewardship over all that God entrusts to us in life is foundational to giving. All that we have, we enjoy because of God's grace and goodness. He has put into our hands the administration of all that He owns. As your preeminent Master, He holds you accountable for how well you manage what He has entrusted to your care (Matthew 25:14–30; Romans 14:12).

This divine perspective helps us understand much of our purpose for living as Christians. We are here to glorify God through the wise investment of our time, our talents, and our treasure. Our Lord came to seek and to save the lost. He has commanded us to continue His mission by helping to fulfill the Great Commission in our generation.

My goal is to help you fulfill God's purpose for your life by showing you the biblical way to invest wisely in God's kingdom and thereby increase your fruitfulness for Christ.

Be Faithful

Faithfulness is another quality that will equip you for your adventure in giving. The apostle Paul says, "It is required that those who have been given a trust must prove faithful" (1 Corinthians 4:2). Faithfulness is dependability—a steady, day-by-day obedience to God in what He has given you to do.

A trustworthy steward will evaluate his opportunities and invest what God has given him in such a way that it will produce the best possible results.

Adopt a Godly Attitude

The attitude of a steward is vital. Paul admonishes, "Each man should give what he has decided in his heart to give, not reluctantly or under compulsion, for God loves a cheer-ful giver" (2 Corinthians 9:7).

The Greek word translated "cheerful" is *hilaros*, from which we get the word "hilarious." Supernatural, Holy Spirit–directed stewardship is giving with expectation, excitement, joy, praise—even laughter. Indeed, God prizes "hilarious givers" because they are the ones who have discovered the exciting adventure of giving.

Recognize and Fulfill Your Stewardship Responsibilities

One of the major responsibilities—and privileges—of a fruitful steward is to share the life-changing message of God's love and forgiveness through Jesus Christ. Our Lord has given to every Christian the command to "Go into all the world and preach the Good News to everyone, everywhere" (Mark 16:15, TLB) and to "make disciples in all the nations" (Matthew 28:19, TLB). This command, which the church has historically called the Great Commission, is the privilege and duty of every man and woman in every generation who confesses Christ as Savior and Lord.

If you and I and Christians everywhere will simply obey our Lord's call to the stewardship of our time, talents, and treasure, we will release not only vast sums of money to advance His kingdom, but all other resources needed to reach billions of people for Christ, and thus help fulfill the Great Commission in this generation.

Matthew 6:21 records perhaps the simplest truth about your commitment:

Where your treasure is, there your heart will be also.

One can determine much about a Christian's spiritual life and how faithfully he fulfills his stewardship responsibilities by what he treasures. Your use of time, talent, and money clearly shows your spiritual commitment because you invest in what your heart values most.

Enjoying God's Abundant Blessings

*G*iving by faith is meant by God to be an exciting privilege. When you honor and praise God through your commitment and obedience to stewardship, He showers you with joy. He turns your giving into a thrilling adventure in Christian living.

Would you like to enjoy such an experience?

Let me share six steps you can take to appropriate God's abundant blessings through your faithful stewardship.

Recognize That Everything You "Own" Actually Belongs to God

All that we have, we possess by the grace and gift of God. Everything belongs to Him. The psalmist records, "The earth is the Lord's, and everything in it, the world, and all who live in it" (Psalm 24:1). God's ownership is eternal and unchanging. He never has given up this right—and never will.

As Christian stewards we must realize that in Christ "we live and move and have our being" (Acts 17:28). Jesus Christ created us (Colossians 1:16). He bought us with His precious blood (1 Peter 1:18,19). And God anointed Him as our Lord (Acts 2:36) and placed everything under His authority (Ephesians 1:20–23). Thus, the whole of our life— our personality, influence, material substance, everything —is His, even our successes (Isaiah 26:12).

God has placed in our trust a measure of time, a unique set of talents, and sufficient treasure to carry out His will for our lives. Our task as faithful stewards is to manage those blessings to bring the maximum glory to His name.

Realize That It Is More Blessed to Give Than to Receive

The Book of Acts records the words of the Lord Jesus, "It is more blessed to give than to receive" (Acts 20:35). I first heard this as a boy, then as an agnostic and later as a young Christian. At that time, I could not comprehend how giving could be better than receiving. Now that I have been a Christian for many years, I truly understand from my own experience and through observing many others why it is "more blessed to give" than to receive.

Giving produces abundance. When you give freely of your-self and of your possessions as a material expression of your spiritual obedience to Christ, God in turn meets your needs abundantly (Luke 6:38). This is true whether you are rich or poor, whether you serve God in a land that is blessed with great material wealth or in a poverty-stricken part of the world. The apostle Paul records:

> *If you give little, you will get little. A farmer who plants just a few seeds will get only a small crop, but if he plants much, he will reap much. Every one must make up his own mind as to how much he should give. Don't force anyone to give more than he really wants to, for cheerful givers are the ones God prizes. God is able to make it up to you by giving you everything you need and more, so that there will not only be enough for your own needs, but plenty left over to give joyfully to others.*

> *For God, who gives seed to the farmer to plant, and later on, good crops to harvest and eat, will give you more and more seed to plant and will make it grow so that you can give away more and more fruit from your harvest.*

> *Yes, God will give you much so that you can give away much, and when we take your gifts to those who need them they will break out into thanksgiving and praise to God for your help* (2 Corinthians 9:6–8,10,11, TLB).

Most Christians have not learned to give, either out of their abundance or out of their poverty and, therefore, are not experiencing the reality of that promise. As a result, they feel unfulfilled and don't understand why.

You can never outgive God. It is a law of God that His blessings back to you always greatly exceed what you give to Him.

The truths of God's holy, inspired Word are universal. The principle of abundant blessing is not just for the rich and famous or for those who live in a land of wealth and opportunity; it is for everyone everywhere who obeys God and follows the principles of giving recorded in His Word. I will share more on this later.

Giving begins an endless circle of joy. God gives; you receive. You give; He receives. He then multiplies your gift back to you in the form of additional supply. It is important to remember that God is the one who initiates this process of blessing. The purpose of the return is not just to reward you for giving, but to increase your ability to give more, thus completing the circle again and again (2 Corinthians 9:10).

Although God owns all the wealth in the universe, few people are willing to share the portion of resources that He has entrusted to them. When someone does begin to give, God releases additional abundance to them so they can give even more. If we break this process on the receiving end of the circle, He is likely to look for someone else He can trust and through whom He can channel His blessings. The Book of Proverbs records:

> *One man gives freely, yet gains even more; another withholds unduly, but comes to poverty. A generous man will prosper; he who refreshes others will himself be refreshed* (Proverbs 11:24,25).

My good friend Don Preston considers himself an average person. At the age of 12, he found his first job working in a small grocery store after school. From the beginning, he gave at least 10 percent of his income to the work of the Lord. Through the years, Don worked hard, and God blessed him abundantly.

Don married young, and he and his wife reared their three children while Don grew in his career. At age 29, after eleven years of managing supermarket meat departments, he began his own wholesale/retail meat business. At that time, he and his family made a decision to give at least 15 percent of their $6,000 yearly earnings to the Lord.

God began to increase their income immediately from $6,000 to $21,000, then to $37,000, $62,000, $85,000, $100,000, and more a year.

"Fifteen years later we sold the meat business to a larger company, wrapped up our assets in nice, neat investments, and went into self-supported Christian ministry for two years," Don says. "We later heard of the evangelistic work of Christian nationals in foreign countries. Their work is flourishing, and it takes little to maintain national families in full-time ministry compared to our own—less than $100 per month in some countries.

"A little fast meat-market math convinced me that I could go back into business, earn money to support these nationals, and multiply myself fifty to one hundred times. By giving $50,000 a year, I could contribute a million dollars to God's work within just twenty years."

With his family's enthusiastic support, Don put aside his plans to join the staff of Campus Crusade for Christ and began instead to pursue this twenty-year course of earning to give. This time around, he and his son started a machinery business in Greenville, South Carolina, and true to his commitment, Don began giving away 50 percent of his income, paying 33 percent in taxes and living modestly on the rest.

Things worked out much better than he expected. He fulfilled his million-dollar commitment in just ten years, channeling the bulk of his funds into *NewLife2000*®, a comprehensive plan for world evangelism designed to help reach the billions who have not yet heard about Christ.[2]

Don's wife, Virginia, died in 1987. Now he and his second wife, Jeanne, have begun to work on a second million to give to the work of the Lord, and their goal is to find a hundred or more other men and women who will do the same.

God's promise in Proverbs 11:24,25 is for everyone. Whether rich or poor, you too can give to receive to give to receive to give again. God knows your heart and whether He can trust you to end the process, as Don Preston emphasizes, on the right word: *give*.

Permit me to share a word of caution here. Do not be disappointed if God doesn't provide you with an immediate financial return as He did with Deborah or Don. The various possibilities of God's blessings are endless. He may have a different plan for you. God knows your true needs, and you must give Him the freedom to do His very best work in your life. He may give you improved health and strength to do your work. He may lead you to a better job, help you decrease your expenses, or change your spending habits so you can live better on your present income. Or He may teach you to be content with what you have so you can enjoy a greater sense of fulfillment in life. Paul affirms this:

> *I know what it is to be in need, and I know what it is to have plenty. I have learned the secret of being content in any and every situation, whether well fed or hungry, whether*

---

[2] Don Preston is one of the founders of "History's Handful," a group of one thousand individuals who will give $1 million or more to help fulfill the Great Commission through Campus Crusade for Christ International/*NewLife2000*. See Appendix A for more information about *NewLife2000*.

living in plenty or in want. I can do everything through him who gives me strength (Philippians 4:12,13).

Many Christians misunderstand the meaning of blessing. Like Paul, Job was a man who experienced both prosperity and poverty. True prosperity is living and giving at the level to which God has called you, with all of your needs met by His supply.

Give By Faith

Simply defined, giving by faith is taking God at His Word and giving generously in anticipation of His faithful provision.

The premise of this concept is threefold. First, God is the absolute source of your supply. Second, giving is based on His resources, not your own. Third, Christ is your link to God's inexhaustible riches.

The apostle Paul includes these precepts in his letter to the Christians at Philippi in which he says:

My God shall supply all your need according to His riches in glory by Christ Jesus (Philippians 4:19, NKJ).

Let's look at this verse for a moment.

God shall supply. Living in a humanistic society, it is easy to believe that man is your source of wealth. When in need, it's easy to look to people and institutions for help. Indeed, God uses them in His process of provision, but they are only the instruments—not the source—of your supply.

According to His riches. Our heavenly Father holds the treasures of heaven and earth in His hands. God said, "The world is mine, and all that is in it" (Psalm 50:12). His supply is not based on the size of your need, but on the enormity of His riches and His authority to disburse them. In good times and bad, His reserves remain stable and inexhaustible.

By Christ Jesus. Jesus Christ claimed all authority in heaven and on earth (Matthew 28:18). You claim God's abundant blessings through Christ. Our Lord laid aside His riches in heaven to identify with you in every area of your human need, ultimately dying on the cross for your sins (2 Corinthians 8:9). When Christ returned to His Father, God reinvested Him with all that He had laid aside, including His inexhaustible riches.

Realize That What You Sow, You Will Reap

On the third day of creation God commanded, "Let the earth burst forth with every sort of grass and seed-bearing plant, and fruit trees with seeds inside the fruit, so that these seeds will produce the kinds of plants and fruits they came from" (Genesis 1:11, TLB).

This principle applies spiritually as well as physically. Paul writes, "A man reaps what he sows. The one who sows to please his sinful nature, from that nature will reap destruction; the one who sows to please the Spirit, from the Spirit will reap eternal life" (Galatians 6:7,8).

The apostle makes it clear that the law of sowing and reaping applies to the use of our material goods as well, as previously examined in 2 Corinthians 9. This law embraces four basic principles.

First, *to reap anything, you must first plant a seed.* Whether your gift is measured in cash or goods or any other medium of exchange, whatever you give is a seed that you sow for an expected harvest.

Second, *to reap a bountiful harvest you must sow your best seed.* Merely sowing for the sake of reaping is not enough. God asks for your finest because He uses what you give as the basis of His supply. There is no second best with God. His provision in response to your obedience is perpetually perfect and always abundant. Since He gave you His very best—His only Son—you grieve the Spirit of God when you do not give Him your best.

This means that the best of your life—the best of your time, the best of your talents, the best of your treasure, the best of everything you have—should be on the altar of sacrifice to God.

In some cultures, the seed may be at least the first tenth of one's paycheck. In other societies, the seed may be the first and best of one's produce or other tangible goods (Numbers 18:12). For example, Abraham willingly gave a tenth of all his spoils of war to Melchizedek, the king of Salem and high priest of the Most High God, as a testimony to God's faithfulness in giving him the victory (Genesis 14:17–20). No doubt these spoils included a wide variety of valuable treasures. On another occasion, after Moses sanctified the Tabernacle in the wilderness, the leaders of Israel brought covered wagons drawn by oxen as gifts to the Lord (Numbers 7:1–5).

Third, whatever you give, *you reap according to the amount you sow.* This biblical principle is basic to life and it applies in every culture and economic custom, whether free enterprise, socialism, or a system where tangible goods are bartered.

Our Lord said:

> *If you give, you will get! Your gift will return to you in full and overflowing measure, pressed down, shaken together to make room for more, and running over. Whatever measure you use to give—large or small—will be used to measure what is given back to you* (Luke 6:38, TLB).

Fourth, *an abundant harvest springs from the most fertile soil.* No intelligent farmer would think of planting inferior seed in poorly prepared soil using worn-out equipment. Rather, he would buy the choicest seed and prepare the soil thoroughly with the finest equipment and fertilizers he could afford.

Like planting good seed in fertile ground, your task as a steward is to seek the greatest possible return for the sake of God's kingdom. You cannot appraise good stewardship by the amount of your gifts, but by how wisely you invest your resources. Good stewardship of any gift is determined by how well it reflects the will of God.

In making decisions, I believe in using the "sound mind" principle of Scripture recorded in 2 Timothy 1:7, "God has not given us a spirit of fear, but of power and of love and of a sound mind" (NKJ).

The "sound mind" referred to in this verse means a well-balanced mind that is under the control of the Holy Spirit, "renewed" according to Romans 12:1,2:

> *Therefore, I urge you, brothers, in view of God's mercy, to offer your bodies as living sacrifices, holy and pleasing to God—this is your spiritual act of worship. Do not conform any longer to the pattern of this world, but be transformed by the renewing of your mind. Then you will be able to test and approve what God's will is—his good, pleasing and perfect will.*

There is a vast difference between the inclination of the non-Christian and the worldly believer to use "common sense" and that of the Christ-centered Christian to follow the "sound mind" principle.[3] One depends on the wisdom of man without benefit of God's wisdom and power; the other, having the mind of Christ, receives wisdom and guidance from God moment by moment through faith.

I encourage you to use the "sound mind" principle to help you determine where to invest in Christ's kingdom. Avoid emotional giving. Giving on impulse just for the sake of giving or contributing where your gifts are likely to be misused or wasted is not only poor stewardship, but is also contrary to the will of God and grieves the Spirit. Perhaps you have received requests from organizations inviting you to invest in their various projects. Carefully evaluate the worthiness of the ministry you choose and the sincerity of the

---

[3] For more information on this topic, see Appendix B.

people involved, and respond to the leading of the Holy Spirit.

Don't be afraid to ask questions. Find out the condition of the "soil." Investigate the financial soundness and integrity of the organization soliciting your support; determine what percentage of your donation will actually go to the project and whether your gift will really be used for the glory of God. I also encourage you to evaluate—in terms of discipleship and evangelism—the fruitfulness of the church or other organizations that invite your contributions.

Give to Glorify God

As a steward of God's resources, you have but one purpose: to glorify Him. It is easy to let the day-to-day demands on your finances turn your eyes from this aim unless you clearly define your priorities. God's holy Word does this for you.

Your number one priority is God. Your second priority is your family. Since the family was the first institution formed by our Creator (Genesis 1:27,28), no conflict exists between the preeminence of God and the priority of family. Rather, meeting the needs of your family is a scriptural mandate and an evidence of faith (1 Timothy 5:8; 6:8). It glorifies God when you help nonbelievers see the life-changing power of Jesus Christ as a result of your caring for the poor, the orphans, and the widows, and your gifts of time, talent, and treasure to agencies concerned for the welfare of the community.

But your top priority is to love, obey, and glorify God. Putting God and the fulfillment of our Lord's Great Commission first in your time, talents, and treasure must be the priority goal of your stewardship. This involves giving to the kingdom of God through your local church and mission organizations that faithfully exalt our Lord, proclaim His holy, inspired Word, and actively work toward the fulfillment of the Great Commission. It is poor stewardship to invest resources that God has entrusted to you in any church or mission cause that is not directly related to discipleship, evangelism, and the fulfillment of our Lord's commands, including the Great Commission.

Give From the Heart

Good stewardship involves more than the mere knowledge and application of the principles and priorities of giving. Motives are an essential part of the picture as well.

Godly motives stem from a cheerful, loving heart for God. We give to please God and express our love to Him. We give out of obedience to our Lord's command to lay up treasures in heaven. We give to be a channel of God's abundant resources to a desperately needy world. We give to help fulfill the Great Commission and, thus, help reach the world for Christ (Luke 12:42–44; 2 Corinthians 5:14,15,18,19; Matthew 28:19). Maintaining right motives through the power of the Holy Spirit is essential if we are to accomplish this objective to the glory of God.

Why is it, then, that we so often fail in this goal? It is because we follow our deceitful hearts and live self-centered lives. Bowing to this materialistic world, we fail to use the keys that unlock God's abundant blessings in our lives and, as a result, plunge into financial bondage.

How can you avoid this? In the following pages I want to show you how to manage your finances and release your faith to experience the adventure in giving that God intended for every Christian.

God Wants You to Be Financially Free

*P*erhaps you have seen enticing advertisements in your newspaper or on television promising you financial independence. What a wonderful prospect! Although God has blessed many of His children with wealth, most of us can only dream about financial independence. Financial freedom, however, is for every Christian steward who faithfully follows God's plan for giving, saving, and spending.

Financial freedom means *having enough to provide adequately for your household and to give generously and joyfully to God's work.*

God wants you to be financially free so you can put Him first in your life and be sensitive to His voice, ready to follow Him whenever—and wherever—He leads.

If this is God's plan, why do many Christians live in financial bondage? The reasons are basic. Not understanding or obeying scriptural principles of stewardship, they succumb to the world's philosophy of money. They burden themselves with the material concerns of life and make little or no commitment to God's work.

I believe that materialism is the greatest hindrance to the worldwide propagation of the gospel today. Perhaps in no other area of our lives are we more guilty of rationalizing. When it comes to material possessions, we seem quite capable of not only convincing ourselves that we need them, but that we also deserve them.

This is not to say that we shouldn't enjoy life. In fact, Jesus promised an abundant life to all who trust and obey Him (John 10:10). The Spirit-filled Christian enjoys life more than anyone else. What I am asking you to consider is this: What material possessions in your life are consuming too much of your time in order to secure and maintain them?

Materialism is not just a Western problem. People in all countries and cultures—from New York to Paris to Calcutta to Nairobi to remote villages along the Amazon—wrestle with some form of materialism.

Bailey Marks, vice president for International Affairs for Campus Crusade for Christ, relates a story that illustrates this:

One day a friend of mine was visiting a pastor in a remote African village. His house was very plain. Built of sticks and mud, it had only a dirt floor and its sparse furnishings were crudely constructed.

My friend asked the pastor, "What is one of the most difficult problems you face in your ministry?"

Without hesitation, the pastor slapped his hand on the table and exclaimed, "Materialism! If my people have one pig, they want two. If they have two pigs, they want a cow, or several cows…"

When I first heard the story, I had a good laugh. But then I realized how true this is of all of us.

It is in the faithful stewardship of what God entrusts to you, not materialism, that you find fulfillment and true meaning to life.

Let me share six specific things you can do to ensure financial freedom for you and your family.

Know and Obey God's Will for Investing Your Money

God's will about money is not a mystery. Biblical principles of stewardship give you a clear revelation of His plan. By basing your decisions on these precepts, you will experience lasting financial freedom.

Every investment of your time, talents, and treasure, unless otherwise directed by the Holy Spirit, should be determined by the "sound mind" principle that I mentioned earlier. Additionally, you should seek the wise counsel of godly people who have successfully applied biblical principles in their financial giving.

There will be times in your life, however, when difficult situations arise for which no scriptural principle or human counsel offers specific direction. You may wonder, *Which course should I take? How do I know for sure that my decision is right?* Even then God makes provision for guidance.

The apostle Paul instructs, "Let the peace of Christ rule in your hearts, since as members of one body you were called to peace" (Colossians 3:15). What does this mean?

Peace is a gift and a calling. The Holy Spirit guides you by the presence or absence of peace in your heart. When you make the right decisions, you will sense calm even in circumstances that are very difficult. When your actions do not coincide with His plan, however, you will feel restless and uncertain.

No better way exists for you to know God's will in your financial decisions than to base your actions on the principles of His Word, and then to invite God to guide you with His peace from within.

Breathe Financially

True financial freedom requires spiritual health. For many years, I have taught the principle of "Spiritual Breathing." In Spiritual Breathing, you exhale the impurities of sin by confession. The Bible promises that if you confess your sins to God, He is faithful and just to forgive you and to purify you from all unrighteousness (1 John 1:9).

To confess your sins is to agree with God about your sins. This means you agree that your sins are wrong and grievous to God; you recognize that God has already forgiven your sins through Christ's death and the shedding of His blood on the cross; and you repent (change your attitude)—through the strength of the Holy Spirit, you turn from your sins and change your conduct.

Then, you inhale the purity of God's righteousness by claiming the fullness of His Spirit by faith on the basis of God's *command* in Ephesians 5:18 and His *promise* in 1 John 5:14,15. In this way you invite Him to direct, control, and empower your life.

As Spiritual Breathing sustains your spiritual health, so "Financial Breathing" preserves your financial freedom and well-being.

You exhale financially by confessing your sin of claiming personal ownership of the resources God has entrusted to you and of withholding those resources from God's work—as though, because you earned them, by right they actually belong to you.

You inhale financially by acknowledging His lordship over all of your time, talents, and treasure and by sharing with others the abundance God provides.

This simple act of faith calls for a total, irrevocable commitment to the ownership of God over every area of your life.

Develop a Financial Plan

A written financial plan gives you the framework for your economic decisions and enables you to measure your progress toward financial freedom.

Developing a plan is not difficult. The family budget serves as a starting point. Easily identifying your needs, wants, and desires, the plan provides a vehicle for setting priorities and forming strategic short-range and long-range goals to govern your spending. Furthermore, the budget enables you to think before you buy, thus keeping your spending on target, enabling you to live modestly and effectively manage credit.

Let me suggest a sound approach to accomplish this goal.

In developing a budget, you will need to calculate your normal monthly cost of living, including insurance, plus seasonal expenses such as vacation and Christmas, and long-term needs such as your children's education and your retirement.

Once you have established a budget, make a commitment before the Lord to live on that amount. Of course, the budget may need to be adjusted from time to time to provide for inflation or changes in circumstances.

Any income over and above what you need according to the budget can be designated as surplus. For example, if you receive a special bonus during the year but you already have enough resources to cover your budget, assume that God has given you this to help others or invest in His work. Any salary increases beyond what your needs require can be passed on as well. By setting a limit on personal needs, you will not only begin to enjoy financial freedom, but you will be able to give substantially to the work of the Lord as God blesses you.

I am not suggesting that you set your needs so low that you cannot adequately live in the society in which God has placed you. I caution you, however, to be careful not to mirror the values of those around you for whom increased income automatically means increased spending on self. God doesn't necessarily reward us as we progress in life by allowing us to increase our standard of living without reference to some set guidelines on what our needs are. He blesses us so that we will have enough for our needs with "*plenty* left over to give joyfully to others" (2 Corinthians 9:8, TLB). This would, of course, include laying up treasures in heaven to help fulfill the Great Commission.

Master Your Credit

Good stewardship requires that you live modestly and effectively manage credit.

Paul admonishes, "Let no debt remain outstanding, except the continuing debt to love one another" (Romans 13:8). Many Christian leaders take this to mean that one should never go into debt for anything. I disagree. A young couple will frequently incur monthly obligations while establishing their home. Throughout life, the purchase of expensive items—such as a house or a car—usually requires indebtedness. The real danger does not lie in the provision of needs, but in self-indulgence, poor planning, lack of discipline, and the passion to satisfy one's greeds.

Satan aims to drive Christians into debt so he can drain them with worry or despair and keep them spiritually impotent and fruitless. For this reason, a faithful steward will never obligate himself so that he cannot, through control of his income, pay his debts.

Invest in God's Kingdom

Every Christian should consider how he can give to help win and disciple the largest possible number of people for Christ. But don't be discouraged if you do not have large financial resources to give.

God measures the value of your gift by the total of your resources. As with the widow who gave her two small coins (Luke 21:1–4), He is pleased and honored when you give sacrificially and will supernaturally multiply your gifts to meet your needs as well as the needs of others. God also is pleased when you give generously out of the abundance He has given you. You can use these resources to give strategically to help take the message of Jesus Christ to millions who have not yet received Him.

Let me suggest giving a minimum of 10 percent of your income to the work of the Lord *as a realistic starting point* for a steward who wants to honor and glorify God with the resources with which he has been entrusted.

The practice of giving 10 percent is called "tithing," and is common among many Christians today as a systematic method of giving. The word *tithe* comes from an Old English term simply meaning a *tenth* and usually refers to giving 10 percent of one's income or resources to the kingdom of God. Tithing, or proportional giving of even more, should play a vital role in our stewardship as we seek to obey our Lord's command to help fulfill the Great Commission.

God established the tithe during the Mosaic period of the Old Testament. Many argue against tithing for today on the grounds that we are no longer under the law, which required tithing, but now live by grace. They assert that, if under law the Israelites gave at least a tenth, under grace we should surely do more as God prospers us (1 Corinthians 16:2). On this basis, many advocate proportional giving, but not necessarily a tenth. I agree. For most people, however, a tenth is a good starting point.

Let me illustrate. A friend who was just beginning to experience the reality of his salvation asked his pastor if God would be satisfied with 5 percent of his income instead of 10 percent. The pastor replied, "Would you be satisfied with 50 percent of your salvation and all the other blessings that God has available for you?" From my perspective, *it is unthinkable, in light of Christ's great sacrifice on the cross, that anyone would give less under grace than the Jews gave under the law.* So by tithing, I mean giving at least a tenth of your income or resources to God's work—not as a matter of law, but as an expression of grace.

The provision of God under grace is based on the principle of the harvest: What we sow we will reap (Galatians 6:7). The apostle Paul says, "If you give little, you will get little. A farmer who plants just a few seeds will get only a small crop, but if he plants much, he will reap much" (2 Corinthians 9:6, TLB). Giving too little to the work of the Lord would amount to "robbing God" just as much today as it did in Malachi's time. To the children of Israel, the Lord said:

> *"Will a man rob God? Surely not! And yet you have...robbed me of the tithes and offerings due to me. And so the awesome curse of God is cursing you, for your whole nation has been robbing me.*
>
> *"Bring all the tithes into the storehouse so that there will be food enough in my Temple; if you do, I will open up the windows of heaven for you and pour out a blessing so great you won't have room enough to take it in!"* (Malachi 3:8–10, TLB).

Although Christ has "redeemed us from the curse of the law by becoming a curse for us" (Galatians 3:13), God has His ways of chastening us for lack of giving or rewarding us for faithfulness in stewardship. Consider what He said to the leaders of Judah through the prophet Haggai:

"Why is everyone saying it is not the right time for rebuilding my Temple?" asks the Lord.

His reply to them is this: "Is it then the right time for you to live in luxurious homes, when the Temple lies in ruins? Look at the result: You plant much but harvest little. You have scarcely enough to eat or drink, and not enough clothes to keep you warm. Your income disappears, as though you were putting it into pockets filled with holes!" (Haggai 1:2–6, TLB).

Have you ever had that feeling? You seem to be on a financial treadmill. You are working harder, yet getting farther behind. Your checking account seems to have sprung a leak. God has not changed. In the time of Haggai, He considered it a top priority to reestablish His physical presence among the people of earth by having the people of Israel rebuild His Temple in Jerusalem. In the Church Age in which we live, God's physical presence among mankind is spread as His Church grows and spreads. How does this occur? By evangelism and discipleship, by helping to fulfill the Great Commission in obedience to our Lord's command.

Ask yourself the following questions:

1. What is the greatest thing that has ever happened to me in my entire life?

2. What is the greatest thing I can do to help others?

3. Since our Savior came to seek and to save the lost, is the spread of the gospel still a top priority for God today?

4. Does God expect me, as a Christian, to be involved in spreading the gospel to the world and thus help fulfill the Great Commission?

5. If opportunities to give to evangelism and discipleship exist, does God expect me to give to them?

6. If I ignore the opportunity to give significantly to God's top priorities, is it reasonable to believe that He is well-pleased with me?

7. If He is not well-pleased with me in the way I handle the finances He has entrusted to me, what might He do to get my attention?

Even though we live in an age of grace, the principles of Haggai are still true.

What is the chief end of man? To glorify God and to enjoy Him forever. And how do we glorify God? Jesus explains that in John 15:8: "This is to my Father's glory, that you bear much fruit, showing yourselves to be my disciples."

In other words, the most important thing you and I can do as believers is to invest our time, our talents, and our treasure to help take the most joyful news—the good news of God's love and forgiveness through the Lord Jesus Christ —to everyone who will listen.

Under grace, the love of Christ constrains us. We cannot misuse or abuse our New Testament liberty. We must remain sensitive and accountable to our just and righteous God.

Obedience to His commands in every facet of our lives is the key to experiencing the presence of Christ and the joy of heaven. Jesus says, "The one who obeys me is the one who loves me...I will only reveal myself to those who love me and obey me. The Father will love them too, and we will come to them and live with them" (John 14:21,23, TLB).

Are you experiencing the presence of Christ in your life? Do you know His joy, His love, His peace, the sense of His direction? If not, could it be that you are not obeying His commands? When you withhold the resources that God has entrusted to you for His work, He has little with which to bless you, and your life becomes unfruitful and unhappy.

I personally know of no greater joy than that of being an instrument of God to communicate the good news of the gospel to others. We are not our own anymore; we have been bought with a price, the precious blood of the Lord Jesus Christ. Our time, talents, and treasure are our way of expressing gratitude to our great and glorious God and Father for all that He has done to fill us with His presence.

Since under grace everything we have belongs to God, we tithe—or even give a greater percentage—not as a requirement of law, but as an act of loving obedience and worship. I believe that we disobey God when we ignore our responsibility in giving and stewardship. And just as God disciplines His children under grace when they are disobedient—because He loves them—the unfaithful steward should be prepared for discipline as well. Let me illustrate.

I love my sons dearly. I remember when I first held them in my arms. I felt my heart attach itself to them as I embraced them. But through the years while they were young, I found it necessary to discipline them. On each occasion before and after their punishment, I explained to them that I loved them and that the correction was for their good.

To make sure they understood, I would ask, "Why did I discipline you?"

Each time through their tears they would respond, "Because you love me."

The fact that I reproved them when they were disobedient did not mean that I loved them less, but more.

So it is with obedience in stewardship. It is vital that we do not allow anything to take precedence over giving our tithes and offerings. I would rather miss my meals and not meet other obligations than to rob God—even though I am under grace, even though I know that He loves me, even though I know that my relationship with Him is vastly different from that of Old Testament believers because of

Christ's death and resurrection and His indwelling presence in my life.

To fail in our accountability to God would be a misunderstanding of grace. Jesus said, "You should tithe" (Matthew 23:23, TLB). Since everything we have we enjoy as a gift of God, not returning to the work of the Lord a percentage of what He has given us, as an expression of our gratitude and love, is disobedience and can result in discipline.

Just as in Malachi God promised to abundantly bless Israel for faithfulness in tithing (Malachi 3:10), I believe God will abundantly bless those today who tithe or give more in a regular, systematic way. An attitude of obedience when you tithe—or give generously in a systematic way—softens the soil of your heart for fruitfulness and thereby gives God opportunity to bless you.

I believe this is the spirit of the Malachi principle.

The premise of tithing as an expression of grace is threefold:

First, *tithing acknowledges God as the source and owner of all that we possess.* Tithing performs a role separate from that of unsystematic giving, which suggests that we believe we own all that we possess. Through tithing we acknowledge that God created our increase.

Second, *tithing is a voluntary act of worship.* At Bethel, Jacob said:

> "If God will help and protect me on this journey and give me food and clothes, and will bring me back safely to my father, then I will choose Jehovah as my God! And this memorial pillar shall become a place for worship; and I will give you back a tenth of everything you give me!" (Genesis 28:20–22, TLB).

If you don't already tithe, you too should consider tithing —or giving more—as an act of worship. Through this act, you keep your focus on the heavenly Father and testify to His kindness and generosity toward you.

Third, *tithing teaches us to put God first.* Moses said, "The purpose of tithing is to teach you always to put God first in your lives" (Deuteronomy 14:23, TLB).

Tithing as a systematic plan for consistent giving enables you to circumvent the emotions and situations that would hinder you from being a faithful steward and, thus, from putting God first in your life. This prioritizing releases you from the tyranny of materialism and clears the channel for God's additional and abundant blessings.

Don Myers, Campus Crusade for Christ director of affairs for Southern Africa, relates how he and his wife, Sue, learned to put this principle into effect in their lives.

"During our first two years as Christians, Sue and I devised a plan to become tithers. The plan entailed a one-percent-per-year increase in our giving until we reached the magic 10 percent. Since our giving at that time was an anemic 4 percent, we were looking at a long, laborious process. We tried that plan for two years, but it was like pulling a tooth *slowly!*

"At that point, we made a radical decision to jump our giving from 6 percent to 10 percent in one leap. This proved to be a relatively painless procedure, and it yielded a financial liberty and sense of peace in our marriage beyond our previous experience. We were encouraged to try new 'quantum leaps.'

"As staff members from 1968 to 1972, we managed to maintain a modest 'beyond tithe' level of giving. Then as we prepared for our move to Africa in 1973, we listened to a message at a staff conference that changed our lives. The speaker said that the best faith response to a financial crisis would be to *increase* one's level of stewardship.

"After prayerfully considering this radical principle, we decided to follow it during our Africa career. We encountered severe financial crises on six occasions during the sixteen years we served in Africa. Each time, by faith, we *increased* our level of giving. And each time the Lord solved the crisis. By the time we left Africa, our giving level was 38 percent!"

Does the principle of tithing apply equally to your time and talents as it does to money? I am convinced that it does.

Giving at least 10 percent of your time to God is not a burdensome task. Many of God's children give far more.

Opportunities to devote your time and talents are limitless. Do you sing? Play a musical instrument? Bake? Perhaps you are an executive, a professor, secretary, child care provider, carpenter, landscaper, mechanic, or bookkeeper. Ask God to show you how to use your talents for His glory. And check with your pastor or the leaders of Christian ministries in your area for opportunities to invest your time and talents for the cause of Christ.

I challenge you to give generously of your time and talents as well as your treasure for six months to see how God will multiply the fruit of your gifts in the lives of others. What an exciting privilege to watch your resources touch lost and hurting people around the world for the glory of God!

Give While You Live

Since everything we possess actually belongs to God and He has made us temporary stewards, we do not leave our money behind when we die; we leave God's money. Then someone else assumes responsibility for our estates and reaps the rewards that God intended for us who accumulated the assets in the beginning.

Many Christians work hard and leave their estates to heirs who are unfaithful to their trust. But a faithful steward, after providing for the present and future needs of his family, invests in God's work while he still lives.

A Christian friend recently shared how he had been appointed the executor of a woman's sizable estate and would be responsible to give her money to Christian ministries after her death. Instead, my friend encouraged her to give the money away while she could observe firsthand the benefits of her investments.

They prayed together, and with his counsel and the help of others, she began to give her money to many worthy Christian projects—to missionaries and mission organizations, struggling churches, and Christian schools. As she gave generously, God blessed her abundantly and made the final years of her life the most exciting and fruitful of all.

The principle of giving while we live applies equally to those with modest means as well. God deals with us individually. I cannot suggest your lifestyle nor give you a specific plan for investing in the cause of Christ. But I do urge you to use your resources for the kingdom while you can direct them in the way God leads you instead of relying on the wisdom of your heirs. Consult an attorney, certified public accountant, financial planner, or trust officer for specific information on how you can give your life savings while you are still alive. Only as a last resort should you leave the responsibility for the distribution of your estate to your heirs or executors. By "giving while you live," you will be involved in winning and discipling others for Christ while you are still alive. As a result, our Lord will manifest Himself to you as He promised in John 14:21.

How to Trust God for Your Finances

hanging economic conditions exemplify the instability of finances throughout the world. Instead of placing their trust in the Lord who promised to meet all of their needs, most Christians trust in their investments, savings, and retirement plans to ensure security and happiness—only to find their hopes dashed when financial reverses deplete their assets. Many are wasting their lives trying to achieve financial security in a volatile world.

Our heavenly Father, on the other hand, wants us to enjoy a full, abundant life free from the cares and stresses brought by confidence in money and other material possessions. Rather than trusting in a worldly system that cannot assure our welfare or relying on our own weak capabilities to provide for our needs, He calls us to depend entirely on Him.

Permit me to suggest a plan that will help you release your faith in God and develop your trust in Him for your finances.

Recognize That God Is Worthy of Your Trust

The psalmist wrote, "The words of the Lord are flawless, like silver refined in a furnace of clay, purified seven times" (Psalm 12:6). You can count on God to do as He says because the One who created the heavens and earth and who established the laws that govern the universe actually owns everything and is far more capable of providing for your needs than you could ever imagine. The writer of Proverbs says, "Trust in the Lord with all your heart;…in all your ways acknowledge him, and he will make your paths straight" (Proverbs 3:5,6). I encourage you to make our Lord and His promises the foundation of your financial security.

Realize That God Wants You to Live a Full and Abundant Life

Our Lord promises to give every obedient Christian an overflowing, joyous life regardless of his financial position. Jesus told His followers, "I have come that they may have life, and that they may have it more abundantly" (John 10:10, NKJ). This generous assurance includes financial freedom.

Substitute Faith for Fear

One emotion that can undermine your faith and throw you back into financial bondage is fear. When anxiety over the future grips you, you lose the ability to trust God for your needs.

By obeying God's will for your life, however, you establish your faith firmly and open your life to His abundant blessings.

The apostle Paul records, "God has not given us a spirit of fear…" (2 Timothy 1:7, NKJ). I encourage you to surrender your fear and place your future into His capable hands. Then put into action the principles of God's Word for financial freedom.

Ask God to Supply Your Needs

James observes, "You do not have, because you do not ask God" (James 4:2). Our Lord says, "If you remain in me and my words remain in you, ask whatever you wish, and it will be given you" (John 15:7). Faith requires action. Ask God, as an act of your will, to supply your needs. Then expect Him, as an expression of your faith, to provide for your needs. God's Word says that whatever we ask according to faith and in harmony with His will, He promises to answer (1 John 5:14,15).

Keep Your Heart and Motives Pure

To truly trust in God for your finances, you must also keep your heart and motives pure. Even if you ask by faith, you will fail to receive if you ask out of wrong motives. James also says, "When you ask, you do not receive, because you ask with wrong motives, that you may spend what you get on your pleasures" (James 4:3). I encourage you to "breathe spiritually" when motives displeasing to our Lord creep into your heart. Confess these wrongful attitudes, then claim the power of the Holy Spirit to help you rely on Him to supply your needs.

Take a Step of Faith

Sometimes God requires of us a further step of faith. Dr. Oswald J. Smith, the famous Canadian evangelist and missionary statesman, had a burning, driving passion "to bring back the King through world evangelization." The entire ministry of the People's Church, which he pastored in Toronto, centered on this vision. The high point of each year was the four-week missionary convention. To Dr. Smith, raising support for missions was the prime duty of every individual—children and adults, filing clerks and millionaires, homemakers and retired seniors.

Each year, he would challenge them to decide on a "faith promise," which they felt God would put into their hands to give to missions above their regular giving—even if they could not see a way in their budget. No one received a reminder, and miraculously each year more than the amount promised came in.[4] As a result, tens of millions of dollars have been given to missions through his example and teaching.

A "faith promise" is not a pledge that must be paid. Rather, it is a voluntary "promise" based on your faith in God's ability to supply out of His resources what you cannot give out of your own. You give as God supplies.

Permit me to give another word of caution here: God does not want you to "promise" what you do not yet have as a substitute for giving what He has presently entrusted to you. Your present possessions are a kind of test on whether you are worthy of being entrusted with more and greater resources. While the concept of "faith promise" giving is not explicitly developed in Scripture, it is based on scriptural principles and serves as a practical strategy for designating future resources to God's kingdom.

---

[4] Lois Neely, *Fire in His Bones, the Official Biography of Oswald J. Smith* (Wheaton, IL: Tyndale House Publishers, 1982), pp. 232–33.

As your faith in God and in His love and trustworthiness grows, let me encourage you to prayerfully make a faith promise—one that is greater than you are capable of fulfilling according to your present income. Take God at His word that He will supply from His unlimited resources. Make a generous faith promise to help fulfill the Great Commission through your church or an organization that is committed to this cause.

In taking such a step of faith, you link your finite life with the infinite God—the God of love, power, wisdom, and sufficiency. You begin to draw upon His inexhaustible supply. You become His instrument for helping to change the world.

Recognizing God's Priority for Missions

*A*s I have studied God's Word for the past forty-five years and, together with our staff, have ministered in countries representing 98 percent of the world's population, I am convinced that every individual or church experiencing God's maximum blessing is directly involved in helping to fulfill the Great Commission (John 14:21–24).

I am deeply concerned that so little of the financial blessing that God has given to Christians is used to help reach the billions of men, women, and children who have never heard the name of Jesus.

In Matthew 28:19,20, Jesus gives us a specific command, "Go and make disciples *in all the nations*, baptizing them into the name of the Father and of the Son and of the Holy Spirit, and then teach these new disciples to obey all the commands I have given you; and be sure of this—that I am with you always, even to the end of the world" (TLB). The nations that have the greatest resources to help build God's kingdom have not obeyed this command fully.

Oswald Smith said, "If you see ten men carrying a heavy log, nine of them on one end and one man struggling to carry the other, which end would most need your help? The end with only one man." This illustrates how inequitably the evangelized nations have been using their resources to help fulfill the Great Commission.

For example, the United States has a gross national income of four trillion dollars. Of this, three trillion is personal income and one trillion corporate income. How much of this vast wealth do Americans give to missions? Only .5 percent. Think of it! That's just 50 cents for every one hundred dollars.[5]

In 1990, the Christian world spent 140 billion dollars on its own church budgets and home missions while sending only 7.5 billion overseas. In literature distribution, non-Christian nations received a mere 1 percent of all Christian books and publications; in broadcasting, 99 percent of all Christian radio/TV dollars were spent in evangelized countries.[6] An estimated 95 percent of all money raised for church budgets in North America goes to domestic use, 4.5 percent goes to established missions, while only .5 percent is sent to frontier missions.

This grieves our Lord, and we cannot expect His greatest blessing as individuals or as a church until we fully obey His command to help fulfill the Great Commission throughout the world.

I believe it is an insult to God for a church to give less than 10 percent or a tithe of its budget to foreign missions. More than that, my personal conviction is that from 25 to 50 percent of every church budget should go overseas. Some churches such as the Peoples Church in Toronto and Briarwood Presbyterian Church in Birmingham, Alabama, for

---

[5] Statistics from the U.S. Center for World Missions.

[6] Statistics taken from David B. Barrett and Todd M. Johnson, *Our Globe and How to Reach It* (Birmingham, AL: New Hope, 1990), p. 27.

example, seek to invest at least 50 percent of their resources in missions as an act of obedience to help fulfill the Great Commission around the world.

Imagine how individuals and churches could impact the world if they committed substantial portions of their resources where they are needed most! Generous gifts to foreign missions could help provide God's holy Word, good Christian books, and training materials to introduce to our Savior people who have never heard the name of Jesus. Increased media time could be devoted to broadcasting the gospel into areas that have little or no Christian witness and into countries that are not open to mission groups.

Check your church missions budget to see where an increase in foreign missions could be made. Look for special projects overseas in which you could have an impact in introducing unreached people to Jesus Christ. Then expect God to honor this expression of your faith and obedience to Him to help reach the multitudes on earth with the most joyful news ever announced.

Experiencing the Adventure

Vonette and I are more excited about our Lord and the privilege of serving Him now than when we made a very special commitment to put Him first in our lives over forty-five years ago. By the spring of 1951, while I was in my senior year at Fuller Theological Seminary, a deacon in the First Presbyterian Church of Hollywood, and directing my business interests, we had become increasingly aware that living for Christ and serving Him was our major goal in life. So we decided to sign a contract with our Lord Jesus Christ in which we yielded our lives and all of our material possessions to Him, including the giving of our finances.

As a result, today Vonette and I personally own very little of this world's goods. We are missionaries for our Lord, and like every other staff member with Campus Crusade, we trust God to provide our financial needs each day through godly people whom He impresses to invest in us and our ministry for Him. Although we seldom have more than enough to meet our needs for a few days or weeks at a time, we have always enjoyed the blessings of God that He promised to all who trust and obey Him. We would rather trust *Him* for all of our needs than all the financial institutions of the world combined.

Several years ago, Vonette and I experienced one of the most exciting adventures in giving of our lives. It all started in 1946 when I heard Dr. Oswald Smith challenge approximately one thousand college students and young singles at a Forrest Home student conference to commit their lives to helping fulfill the Great Commission. He asked each of us to place our name on a country and claim it for our Lord through prayer and finances as God would lead—if necessary, even to give our lives to help reach that country for Christ. I put my name on the Soviet Union and began praying for God to do a great and mighty work in that country.

When Vonette and I were married, she joined me in praying for the Soviet Union. In recent years we and our staff have ministered to the Russian people with fantastic results, helping to train thousands of pastors and laymen in various republics of the former Soviet Union.

One day, a Christian leader from the Soviet Union visited our headquarters and asked us to start a New Life Training Center in Moscow. The cost of launching one discipleship training center would be $50,000 for the first year. Later, the thought flashed through my mind: Could God work through me by using my retirement pension to help establish such a training center? My years of praying for the Soviet people and several visits to their country had given me a special love and burden for them. By starting a New Life Training Center with the proceeds of my pension, I could have a rare opportunity to help reach many thousands of them for our dear Lord Jesus Christ! I had no idea how much my pension totalled, but I joyfully considered the prospect.

First, though, I had to discuss my idea with Vonette. After thoroughly listening to what I thought God was leading us to do and asking a few pertinent questions expressing her concerns, she responded enthusiastically. We prayed and agreed to trust the Lord to provide for our older years.

I checked to find out how much money had accumulated in my pension fund. To our amazement, I had almost the exact amount needed to fund the training center for the first year. Joy and excitement still floods my heart today as I share this story with you. The very thought that God could use my retirement pension to help introduce many thousands of people to Christ overwhelms me. I cannot thank God enough for the privilege of making this contribution of my time, talents, and treasure to help fulfill the Great Commission.

Have you made your commitment to help fulfill the Great Commission by investing in Christ's kingdom? He is calling individuals to make radical commitments of their resources to help fulfill the Great Commission in our generation. He reserves a special blessing for those who give generously of their time, talents, and treasure to His work (John 14:21,23).

It is not likely that God will lead you to give your retirement funds for the cause of Christ. He wants to be original with each of us. Vonette and I have simply responded to His particular call on our lives. But for maximum blessing and fruitfulness for the glory of God, you will want to obey His will and leading as you follow His plan for your life.

I urge you to develop a personal strategy for giving that will enable you to invest wisely and significantly in the kingdom of God and thus increase your fruitfulness for Christ. Acknowledge God as the source and owner of your possessions, and be ready to give an account of your stewardship to Him. Offer your gifts to the Lord Jesus as an act of praise and worship. Put God first in your giving. And manage your time, talents, and treasure to bring maximum glory to His name by laying up an abundance of treasures in heaven. In so doing, you too will experience the wonderful adventure of living and giving by faith.

N O T E

Remember, *How You Can Experience the Adventure of Giving* is a transferable concept. You can master it by reading it six times; then pass it on to others as our Lord commands us in Matthew 28:20, "Teach these new disciples to obey all the commands I have given you" (TLB). The apostle Paul encouraged us to do the same: "The things you have heard me say in the presence of many witnesses entrust to reliable men who will also be qualified to teach others" (2 Timothy 2:2).

Self-Study Guide

1. Make a list of people you know who give faithfully to God's work. Ask them to share their experiences of joyful giving.

2. Memorize 1 Thessalonians 5:18 and meditate on it whenever you feel unthankful.

3. Memorize Matthew 6:21. Evaluate your giving and spending habits to see where your treasure lies.

4. Think of an instance in your life that illustrates why giving is better than receiving.

5. Memorize Philippians 4:19. Remind yourself of this verse each time your faith to give is tested.

6. How are you giving your time, talents, and treasure to help fulfill the Great Commission? How do your gifts reflect a desire to see others accept God's love and forgiveness?

7. Prayerfully ask the Holy Spirit to help you set financial priorities. Write them down and review them each time you pay your bills or do your accounting.

8. Examine your giving to missions to see if it reflects the priority you have set for it.

9. In which areas of your life do you feel greedy or materialistic? How do these feelings affect your spiritual well-being?

10. Is there any part of your finances that you have not completely surrendered to God? If so, why? What course of action do you plan to take to correct this matter?

11. List ways to tithe your time and talents. How can you work them into your present schedule?

12. Read 1 John 2:15–17. Describe what you think loving the world means. How can this detract from your godly stewardship? What are the advantages of doing the will of the Father instead?

Group Discussion Questions

1. To encourage one another, share with your group how God has blessed your giving.

2. As a group, study the parable found in Matthew 25:14–29 and list the characteristics you find in the good and bad stewards. Apply these to the way people live today.

3. Share one way in which Satan tempts you to give less. Be specific. How can you overcome this temptation in the future?

4. With your group, list several ways in which you can share your abundance with others in both material and non-material ways.

5. Suppose a new Christian confides in you that he is afraid to give God control over his giving. How would you advise him?

Appendix A

NewLife2000

NewLife2000 is a comprehensive plan for world evangelism designed to help fulfill the Great Commission.

We have divided the world into 5,000 ministry regions, one for each population area of approximately one million people. The plan calls for establishing a New Life Training Center in each of these regions. Each Training Center—directed and staffed by highly trained, Spirit-filled local national Christians—will have its own tailor-made, culturalized ministry strategy to coordinate the work of evangelism and discipleship in its area.

The strategy includes the use of the *JESUS* film, an ongoing program of leadership training, and other evangelistic efforts to give everyone in the region a chance to say "yes" to Christ.

The plan for each main population area also calls for planting hundreds of New Life Groups, ranging in size from ten to thirty people and composed largely of new Christians. Those who respond to the gospel will be brought into the fellowship of these small groups. The New Life Training Center will provide further discipling with emphasis on "spiritual multiplication" in accordance with 2 Timothy 2:2.

The goals of *NewLife2000* are to:

- Present the gospel to more than 6 billion people by the year 2000
- Introduce at least 1 billion people to faith in Jesus Christ
- Start 10 million New Life Groups
- Involve 200 million new Christians in New Life Groups
- Train millions of leaders through 5,000 New Life Training Centers

- Establish discipleship and training ministries on 8,000 campuses worldwide to help introduce millions of college students and their professors to Christ
- Help establish more than 1 million churches in cooperation with thousands of churches of all Christian denominations
- Assist local churches and individuals in adopting one or more of the 5,000 New Life Training Centers at an average cost of $50,000 per center

Christians from North America, Europe, and more than 150 nations around the world are a part of *NewLife2000*. These men and women from diverse backgrounds include pastors, students, businessmen, homemakers, diplomats, prisoners, farmers, athletes, executives, and military leaders. Millions of believers within thousands of churches, denominations, organizations, and mission agencies are uniting to make *NewLife2000* a priority for their evangelism and discipleship ministries at home and abroad.

Campus Crusade for Christ is seeking to recruit tens of thousands of full-time workers and trained volunteers to give leadership to the New Life Training Centers and the *JESUS* film teams, to communicate the gospel to more than 6 billion people by the year 2000.

Appendix B

Maximizing Your Life According to the "Sound Mind" Principle of Scripture

Now that you have started on your thrilling adventure of giving by faith and have begun developing a personal strategy for investing in God's kingdom, you will discover many seemingly effective avenues in which to give of your time, talents, and treasure. Suddenly, you may find yourself confused about how to wisely use the resources God has entrusted to you among so many exciting choices. How does a sincere steward discover God's will for the investment of his time, talents, and treasure? By applying the "sound mind" principle of Scripture. Let me explain.

In 2 Timothy 1:7 the apostle Paul writes, "God has not given us a spirit of fear, but of power and of love and of a sound mind" (NKJ). The "sound mind" referred to in this verse means a well-balanced mind that is under the control of the Holy Spirit, "renewed" according to Romans 12:1,2:

Therefore, I urge you, brothers, in view of God's mercy, to offer your bodies as living sacrifices, holy and pleasing to God—this is your spiritual act of worship. Do not conform any longer to the pattern of this world, but be transformed by the renewing of your mind. Then you will be able to test and approve what God's will is—his good, pleasing and perfect will.

Let me ask you: Do you make your decisions according to the "sound mind" principle?

If you would like to know the will of God for your life according to the "sound mind" principle, consider these questions: First, *Why did Jesus come?* He came "to seek and to save what was lost" (Luke 19:10). Then, *What is the greatest experience of your life?* If you are a Christian, your answer quite obviously will be, "Coming to know Christ personally as my Savior and Lord." Finally, *What is the greatest thing you can do to help others?* The answer again is obvious, "Introduce them to Christ."

Thus, every sincere Christian will want to make his God-given time, talents, and treasure available to Christ so that his fullest potential will be realized for Him. For one Christian, this talent may be prophetic preaching, evangelism, or teaching; for another, it may be business; for another, the ministry or missions; for another, homemaking.

As you evaluate the talents God has given you, may I suggest that you take a sheet of paper and list the most logical ways through which your life can be used to accomplish the most for the glory of God. List the pros and cons of each opportunity. Prayerfully consider where or how, according to the "sound mind" principle, the Lord Jesus Christ can accomplish the most in continuing His great ministry of seeking and saving the lost. Such a procedure will inevitably result in positive actions leading to God's perfect will for your life. But note a word of caution. The "sound mind" principle is not valid unless certain factors exist:

- There must be no unconfessed sin in your life.

- Your life must be fully dedicated to Christ, and you must be filled with the Holy Spirit in obedience to the command of Ephesians 5:18.

- You must walk in the Spirit (abide in Christ) moment by moment, placing your faith in the trustworthiness of God with the confidence that the Lord is directing and will continue to direct your life according to His promises in Scripture.

The counsel of others should be prayerfully considered, especially that of mature, dedicated Christians who know the Word of God and are able to properly relate the Scriptures to your need. However, be careful not to make the counsel of others a "crutch." Although God often speaks to us through other Christians, we are admonished to place our trust in Him (Proverbs 3:5).

When discussing God's will, there are four basic factors to consider, somewhat similar to the "sound mind" principle. God's will is revealed in the following:

1) His Word

2) Providential circumstances

3) Conviction based upon reason

4) Impressions of the Holy Spirit upon our minds

However, such an appraisal is safer with a mature believer than with a new or worldly Christian, and there is always the danger of misunderstanding impressions.

Know the source of leading before responding to it. To the inexperienced, what appears to be the leading of God may not be from Him at all but from "the rulers of darkness of this world." Satan and his helpers often disguise themselves as "angels of light" by counterfeiting the works of God to deceive His followers.

One further word of caution must be given. It is true that God still reveals His will to some men and women in dramatic ways, but this should be considered the exception rather than the rule.

God still leads today as He has through the centuries. Philip the deacon, for example, was holding a successful campaign in Samaria. The "sound mind" principle would have directed him to continue his campaign. However, God overruled by a special revelation, and Philip was led by the Holy Spirit to preach Christ to the Ethiopian eunuch (Acts 8:26–39). According to tradition, God used the Ethiopian eunuch to communicate the message of our living Lord to his own country.

Living according to the "sound mind" principle allows for such dramatic leadings of God, but we are not to wait for revelations before we start moving for Christ. Faith must have an object. A Christian's faith is built on the authority of God's Word supported by historical fact and is not based on any shallow emotional experience. However, a Christian's trust in God's will revealed in His Word will result in decision-making based on the "sound mind" principle. Usually, the confirmation that you are in God's will is a quiet, peaceful assurance that you are doing what God wants you to do with the expectancy that God will use you to "bear much fruit."

The result of a life that is lived according to the "sound mind" principle is the most joyful, abundant, and fruitful life of all.

Expect the Lord Jesus Christ to draw men to Himself through you. As you begin each day, acknowledge the fact that you belong to Him. Thank Him for the fact that He lives within you. Invite Him to use your mind to think His thoughts, your heart to express His love, your lips to speak His truth. Ask Jesus to be at home in your life and to walk around in your body in order that He may continue seeking and saving souls through you.

It is my sincere prayer that you may know this kind of life, that you may fully appropriate all that God has given you as your rightful heritage in Christ.

Fasting & Prayer

In 1994, I felt led by God to undergo a 40-day fast. During that time, God impressed on me that He was going to send a great spiritual awakening to America, and that this revival would be preceded by a time of spiritual preparation through repentance, with a special emphasis on fasting and prayer. In 2 Chronicles 7:14, God gives us a promise of hope that involves repentance:

If my people, who are called by my name, will humble themselves and pray and seek my face and turn from their wicked ways, then will I hear from heaven and will forgive their sin and will heal their land.

Fasting is the only spiritual discipline that meets all the conditions of 2 Chronicles 7:14. When a person fasts, he humbles himself; he has more time to pray; he has more time to seek God's face, and certainly he would turn from all known sin. One could read the Bible, pray, or witness for Christ without repenting of his sins. But one cannot enter into a genuine fast with a pure heart and pure motive and not meet the conditions of this passage.

Because of this promise, God has led me to pray that at least two million North Americans will fast and pray for forty days for an awakening in America and the fulfillment of the Great Commission. As millions of Christians rediscover the power of fasting as it relates to the holy life, prayer, and witnessing, they will come alive. Out of this great move of God's Spirit will come the revival for which we have all prayed so long, resulting in the fulfillment of the Great Commission.

I invite you to become one of the two million who will fast and pray for forty days. Also, I encourage you to attend the Fasting & Prayer gatherings held each year. If you feel God leading you to participate, please let us know on the Response Form. For more information, see the Resources or call (800) 888-FAST.

Other Resources by Bill Bright

Resources for Fasting and Prayer

The Coming Revival: America's Call to Fast, Pray, and "Seek God's Face." This inspiring yet honest book explains how the power of fasting and prayer by millions of God's people can usher in a mighty spiritual revival and lift His judgment on America. *The Coming Revival* can equip Christians, their churches, and our nation for the greatest spiritual awakening since the first century.

7 Basic Steps to Successful Fasting and Prayer. This handy booklet gives practical steps to undertaking and completing a fast, suggests a plan for prayer, and offers an easy-to-follow daily nutritional schedule.

Preparing for the Coming Revival: How to Lead a Successful Fasting and Prayer Gathering. In this easy-to-use handbook, the author presents step-by-step instructions on how to plan and conduct a fasting and prayer gathering in your church or community. The book also contains creative ideas for teaching group prayer and can be used for a small group or large gatherings.

The Transforming Power of Fasting and Prayer. This follow-up book to *The Coming Revival* includes stirring accounts of Christians who have participated in the fasting and prayer movement that is erupting across the country.

Resources for Group and Individual Study

Five Steps of Christian Growth. This five-lesson Bible study will help group members be sure that they are a Christian, learn what it means to grow as a Christian, experience the joy of God's love and forgiveness, and discover how to be filled with the Holy Spirit. Leader's and Study Guides are available.

Five Steps to Sharing Your Faith. This Bible study is designed to help Christians develop a lifestyle of introducing others to Jesus Christ. With these step-by-step lessons, believers can learn how to share their faith with confidence through the power of the Holy Spirit. Leader's and Study Guides are available.

Five Steps to Knowing God's Will. This five-week Bible study includes detailed information on applying the Sound Mind Principle to discover God's will. Both new and more mature Christians will find clear instructions useful for every aspect of decision-making. Leader's and Study Guides are available.

Five Steps to Making Disciples. This effective Bible study can be used for one-on-one discipleship, leadership evangelism training in your church, or a neighborhood Bible study group. Participants will learn how to begin a Bible study to disciple new believers as well as more mature Christians. Leader's and Study Guides are available.

Ten Basic Steps Toward Christian Maturity. These time-tested Bible studies offer a simple way to understand the basics of the Christian faith and provide believers with a solid foundation for growth. The product of many years of extensive development, the studies have been used by thousands. Leader's and Study Guides are available.

Introduction: The Uniqueness of Jesus
Step 1: The Christian Adventure
Step 2: The Christian and the Abundant Life
Step 3: The Christian and the Holy Spirit
Step 4: The Christian and Prayer
Step 5: The Christian and the Bible
Step 6: The Christian and Obedience

Step 7: The Christian and Witnessing
Step 8: The Christian and Giving
Step 9: Exploring the Old Testament
Step 10: Exploring the New Testament

A Handbook for Christian Maturity. This book combines the *Ten Basic Steps* Study Guides in one handy volume. The lessons can be used for daily devotions or with groups of all sizes.

Ten Basic Steps Leader's Guide. This book contains teacher's helps for the entire *Ten Basic Steps* Bible Study series. The lessons include opening and closing prayers, objectives, discussion starters, and suggested answers to the questions.

Resources for Christian Growth

Transferable Concepts. This series of time-tested messages teaches the principles of abundant Christian life and ministry. These "back-to-the-basics" resources help Christians grow toward greater spiritual maturity and fulfillment and live victorious Christian lives. These messages, available in book format and on video or audio cassette, include:

How You Can Be Sure You Are a Christian
How You Can Experience God's Love and Forgiveness
How You Can Be Filled With the Spirit
How You Can Walk in the Spirit
How You Can Be a Fruitful Witness
How You Can Introduce Others to Christ
How You Can Help Fulfill the Great Commission
How You Can Love By Faith
How You Can Pray With Confidence
How You Can Experience the Adventure of Giving

A Man Without Equal. This book explores the unique birth, life, teachings, death, and resurrection of Jesus Christ and shows how He continues to change the way we live and think today. Available in book and video formats.

Life Without Equal. This inspiring book shows how Christians can experience pardon, purpose, peace, and power for living the Christian life. The book also explains how to release Christ's resurrection power to help change the world.

Have You Made the Wonderful Discovery of the Spirit-Filled Life? This booklet shows how you can discover the reality of the Spirit-filled life and live in moment-by-moment dependence on God.

The Holy Spirit: Key to Supernatural Living. This booklet helps you enter into the Spirit-filled life and explains how you can experience power and victory.

Promises: A Daily Guide to Supernatural Living. These 365 devotionals will help you remain focused on God's great love and faithfulness by reading and meditating on His promises each day. You will find your faith growing as you get to know our God and Savior better.

Resources for Evangelism

Witnessing Without Fear. This best-selling, Gold Medallion book offers simple hands-on, step-by-step coaching on how to share your faith with confidence. The chapters give specific answers to questions people most often encounter in witnessing and provide a proven method for sharing your faith.

Reaching Your World Through Witnessing Without Fear. This six-session video provides the resources needed to sensitively share the gospel effectively. Each session begins with a captivating dramatic vignette to help viewers apply the training. Available in individual study and group packages.

Have You Heard of the Four Spiritual Laws? This booklet is one of the most effective evangelistic tools ever developed. It presents a clear explanation of the gospel of Jesus Christ, which helps you open a conversation easily and share your faith with confidence.

Would You Like to Know God Personally? Based on the *Four Spiritual Laws*, this booklet uses a friendly, conversational format to present four principles for establishing a personal relationship with God.

Jesus and the Intellectual. Drawing from the works of notable scholars who affirm their faith in Jesus Christ, this booklet shows that Christianity is based on irrefutable historic facts. Good for sharing with unbelievers and new Christians.

A Great Adventure. Written as from one friend to another, this booklet explains how to know God personally and experience peace, joy, meaning, and fulfillment in life.

Resources by Vonette Bright

The Joy of Hospitality: Fun Ideas for Evangelistic Entertaining. Co-written with Barbara Ball, this practical book tells how to share your faith through hosting barbecues, coffees, holiday parties, and other events in your home.

The Joy of Hospitality Cookbook. Filled with uplifting Scriptures and quotations, this cookbook contains hundreds of delicious recipes, hospitality tips, sample menus, and family traditions that are sure to make your entertaining a memorable and eternal success. Co-written with Barbara Ball.

Beginning Your Journey of Joy. This adaptation of the *Four Spiritual Laws* speaks in the language of today's women and offers a slightly feminine approach to sharing God's love with your neighbors, friends, and family members.

These and other products from Campus Crusade for Christ are available from your favorite bookseller or by calling (800) 235-7255 (within U.S.) or (770) 631-9940 (outside U.S.).

 BILL BRIGHT is founder and president of Campus Crusade for Christ International. Serving in 172 major countries representing 98 percent of the world's population, he and his dedicated team of more than 113,000 full-time staff, associate staff, and trained volunteers have introduced tens of millions of people to Jesus Christ, discipling millions to live Spirit-filled, fruitful lives of purpose and power for the glory of God.

Response Form

○ I have received Jesus Christ as my Savior and Lord as a result of reading this book.

○ I am a new Christian and want to know Christ better and experience the abundant Christian life.

○ I want to be one of the two million people who will join you in forty days of fasting and prayer for revival.

○ I have completed an extended or forty-day fast with prayer and am enclosing my written testimony to encourage and bless others.

○ Please send me *free* information on staff and ministry opportunities with Campus Crusade for Christ.

○ Please send me *free* information about other books, booklets, audio cassettes, and videos by Bill and Vonette Bright.

NAME

ADDRESS

CITY   STATE   ZIP

COUNTRY

Please check the appropriate box(es), clip, and mail this form in an envelope to:

> Campus Crusade for Christ
> 375 Hwy 74 South, Suite A
> Peachtree City, GA 30269

You may also fax your response to (800) 514-7072, or send E-mail to nlrrep@campuscrusade.org. Visit our website at www.campuscrusade.org.